The School Segregation Cases

THE SCHOOL
SEGREGATION CASES

A system of "separate but equal" public schools was required by law in seventeen of the United States for over fifty years. Segregation of the races was supported by a famous Supreme Court decision (*Plessy* v. *Ferguson*, 1896), which held that such separation did not imply the inferiority of either group. From 1930 to 1950 civil rights leaders fought to bring black schools up to the level of the whites' schools. But in 1950, they shifted to an effort to end not inequality, but segregation itself. Five suits were brought in lower courts. All but one were lost, and all were appealed to the U.S. Supreme Court. The Court, using *Brown* v. *Board of Education of Topeka* as the title case, finally gave its ruling on May 17, 1954, in a decision that would affect the nation's schools for many subsequent years.

THE PRINCIPALS

THE PLAINTIFFS:

Parents and pupils in the black schools of Clarendon County, South Carolina; Prince Edward County, Virginia; Topeka, Kansas; Hockessin and Claymont, Delaware; and Washington, D.C. Organizers of NAACP branches in these communities, like Rev. Francis Griffin, Rev. Joseph Delaine, Billy Fleming, M. L. Burnett, and Elisha Scott.

Leading figures: Barbara Johns, Silas Fleming, Mrs. Lucinda Todd, Katherine Carper.

THE LAWYERS:

Thurgood Marshall, Robert L. Carter, and Jack Greenberg of the NAACP national legal staff. Oliver Hill and Spottswood W. Robinson III of Virginia; Charles Bledsoe, Charles and John Scott of Topeka; Louis L. Redding of Wilmington; George E. C. Hayes and James M. Nabrit, Jr., of Washington, D.C.

THE JUDGES:

Of the Supreme Court of the United States: Chief Justice Earl Warren; Associate Justices Felix Frankfurter, Hugo Black, Robert Jackson.

Of the lower courts: Judge J. Waites Waring of South Carolina; Judge Walter Huxman of Kansas; Chancellor Collins J. Seitz of Delaware.

THE EXPERTS:

More than forty psychologists, psychiatrists, sociologists, educators, and other social scientists who testified on the effects of segregation on children of both races.

Leading figures: Henry Garrett (for the defense); Kenneth Clark; Frederic Wertham; Otto Klineberg; Jerome Bruner; Robert Redfield; David Krech; Louisa Holt (for the plaintiffs).

Historians: C. Vann Woodward and John Hope Franklin.

ROSTER OF LEGAL PARTICIPANTS
IN THE SCHOOL CASES
BEFORE THE U.S. SUPREME COURT

APPEARING IN 1952:

Robert L. Carter for plaintiffs; Paul E. Wilson for defendants (*Brown v. Board of Education of Topeka*)

Thurgood Marshall for plaintiffs; John W. Davis for defendants (*Briggs* v. *Elliott*)

Spottswood W. Robinson III for plaintiffs; T. Justin Moore for defendants (*Davis* v. *County School Board*—Virginia)

George E. C. Hayes and James M. Nabrit, Jr., for plaintiffs; Milton Korman for defendants (*Bolling* v. *Sharpe*—District of Columbia)

Louis L. Redding and Jack Greenberg for plaintiffs; H. Albert Young for defendants (*Bulah* v. *Gebhart* and *Belton* v. *Gebhart*—Delaware)

BRIEFS SUBMITTED IN 1953 BY

Robert L. Carter
Thurgood Marshall
Spottswood W. Robinson III
Louis L. Redding
Jack Greenberg
Harold R. Boulware
Oliver W. Hill
Charles S. Scott

(N.B. The District of Columbia case is now considered as a separate one and the briefs by Hayes and Nabrit are not included under *Brown*.)

OF COUNSEL IN *Brown*:

George E. C. Hayes
James M. Nabrit, Jr.
John Scott
Constance Baker Motley
Charles Black
Elwood Chisholm
William Coleman
Charles Duncan
William Will
David Pinsky
Frank D. Reeves
Jack Weinstein

A FOCUS BOOK

The School Segregation Cases

*(Brown v.
Board of Education
of Topeka
and others)*

*The United States
Supreme Court Rules
on Racially Separate
Public Education*

by Janet Stevenson

FRANKLIN WATTS, INC.
NEW YORK/1973

*The authors and publishers of the Focus Books
wish to acknowledge the helpful editorial
suggestions of Professor Richard B. Morris.*

Photos from United Press International:
pp. 6, 11, 20, 45, 51, 52, 55.

Library of Congress Cataloging in Publication Data

Stevenson, Janet.
    The school segregation cases.

    (A Focus book)
    SUMMARY: Details the events resulting in the
court cases which led to the 1954 Supreme Court
decision decreeing school integration.
    Bibliography: p.
    1. Segregation in education–Law and legislation–
United States–Juvenile literature. [1. Segregation in
education–Law and legislation] I. Title.
KF4155.Z9S74   344'.73'0798   73-5722
ISBN 0-531-01046-5

Contents

Prince Edward County 1

Clarendon County 16

The Sweatt and McLaurin Cases 19

Briggs v. *Elliott* 27

Brown v. *Board of Education of Topeka* 33

The Other School Cases 42

Two Supreme Court Decisions 47

Bibliography of Sources 58

Index 59

Prince Edward County

In the middle of the morning—a sunny Monday morning in April 1951—the phone rang in the office of the principal of an all-black high school in the southwestern part of Virginia.

A voice that sounded to the principal as if it were disguised told Boyd Jones that two of his Moton High School students were at the Greyhound Bus station in Farmville and would be in trouble with the police unless he came and got them right away. Before Principal Jones could ask who was speaking, the person at the other end of the line hung up.

Jones hesitated a few moments before deciding whether or not to investigate. As soon as the weather turned warm in the spring, there was a temptation to cut school, and he had often warned Moton students that anyone who did was on his own. The police were supposed to arrest any truant they could catch. If this mysterious phone call just meant that a couple of boys were breaking the school attendance law, it was not worth following up. But it had sounded more serious. Even in the quiet back-country, where racial tensions were lower than in the cities, there was always the chance that a teen-age prank by black students would be misinterpreted and would lead to an unpleasant incident of some sort.

At last, reluctantly, Boyd Jones put aside the work he had laid out on his desk, got into his car, and drove the few miles into "downtown" Farmville. He circled the block where the bus terminal was located, looking for signs of trouble or any familiar young black face. But he saw no one and nothing out of the ordinary.

Two white policemen were sitting in a car parked near the bus station. Jones asked if they had seen any Moton students. They hadn't. Neither had they heard of any trouble. The principal was beginning to wonder if someone was playing a joke on him, but having come this far, he decided to check things out completely. So he parked his car and went into the station. There were no Moton students inside, and the ticket agent said he hadn't seen any.

Asking questions like this in a little town—Farmville's population was less than 5,000 at the time—was a good way to start rumors flying. So Jones decided to let the matter drop. Still puzzling over why he had been tricked and by whom, he headed his car back toward the high school.

The entire trip had taken less than an hour. But in that brief time an event had taken place that was going to change the life of Boyd Jones and the lives of the students of Moton High School and the inhabitants of Prince Edward County—black and white, young and old—and in the end, of the citizens of the state of Virginia and of the United States: all those whose lives were affected by the system of public schools.

As soon as the principal's car had left the parking lot, a signal had been given inside the school. Notes were passed out to four student messengers, who delivered them to all the classrooms in the building. They were the usual typed announcements of a school assembly, and they were signed with the usual initials—B.J.

Teachers who received the notes assumed they had been signed by Boyd Jones. They dismissed their classes and followed their students to the auditorium, where folding chairs were being set up by some of the senior students. In less than a quarter of an hour the whole student body of 450 was seated and waiting to hear why the assembly had been called. A few of the student leaders were seen disappearing behind the curtains that hid the stage. Then, those curtains were pulled and there—instead of Boyd Jones—stood a pretty, petite, senior girl named Barbara Johns.

It was she who had signed the notes and who now took charge of this most unusual assembly. Barbara began her speech by asking the teachers present to leave. The meeting, she said, had been called by a student committee and was for students only. Some of the teachers did leave. Others sat in their chairs in a state of mild shock. Finally one man teacher got to his feet to protest. He was forcibly removed by a group of senior boys. After that Barbara had the cooperation of the other teachers and the undivided attention of her fellow students.

She wasted no words reminding them of what they already knew: that conditions at their school were "a blight on the whole community." Moton had been built in the 1930's for 180 students; now it held 450. The overcrowding had been slightly relieved in the forties by building three temporary shacks that looked like chicken coops and that were about as comfortable. Their roofs leaked. They were heated in winter by "drum stoves" that burned wood. Those who sat close were roasted, and those who sat far away shivered and caught cold. The buses that brought black students to Moton were broken-down castoffs from the white school.

The parents and teachers of Prince Edward County had been trying for almost three years to persuade the Farmville School Board to make major improvements or, even better, to build a new black high school. The school board admitted the need, but said it had no money. The state of Virginia offered $50,000 on condition that the local board contribute the same amount. But the board said that didn't help. There would have to be a bond issue to raise the $50,000 and higher taxes to repay it. White taxpayers weren't going to be willing to "shell out more money for nigger schools."

What the board said they would do instead was to plan and propose an improvement program for both the white and black schools. They hoped the white taxpayers of Prince Edward County wouldn't notice that blacks would get the use of a bigger share of the money than they contributed in taxes.

The Moton parents were willing to wait for that sort of a solution if it was not going to be too long in coming. The P.T.A. and the new branch of the NAACP * sent delegations to every meeting of the school board to press for a definite date, but they got no satisfaction. Finally, in February, the board said they were trying to buy some land, a few miles out of town, for a new black high school. When the deal was closed, the Moton parents would be notified. In the meantime, they were told, there was no point in their coming to the meetings.

Most of the Moton students knew all this, and knew that the notification had never come. They were ready to agree with Barbara Johns that since polite pressure hadn't worked on Mr. Charley,** it was time to see what would. A committee of student leaders, called together by Barbara, had been meeting in secret for six months. Included were the sons and daughters of both militant and conservative black families; some whose jobs depended on their staying in the good graces of the local white Establishment, and some who owned the land they farmed and were more independent.

The members of the student committee hadn't confided in or asked help from their parents. Nor from their teachers. Nor from Principal Jones. They were convinced that what they were now proposing was in line with what their parents and their teachers had taught them. But they were taking the action on their own.

* The National Association for the Advancement of Colored People.

** A nickname used by southern blacks for whites who are members of the white Establishment, or supporters of it.

[4]

What they were proposing was to refuse to go to school any longer in the dilapidated, tar-paper shacks of Moton.

In other words, to strike for a new school!

At this point in her speech, Barbara took off one of her shoes and used the heel for a gavel. Pounding on one of the benches on the stage, she shouted, "I want you all out of here!" And the students applauded her noisily.

But at that moment, Boyd Jones was walking up the front steps—about twenty minutes before he was expected. He heard what was going on and went straight to the auditorium, where he pleaded with the students not to do what Barbara was asking. "He said that this would not solve our problems. . . . The students didn't boo him. They had a lot of respect for him . . . [but] Barbara asked him to go back to his office, and he finally did." *

"If we go out together and stay together, nobody will be punished," Barbara told the students. There were placards that had been made—secretly—in the school shop, for pickets to carry. Some of the slogans were:

WE WANT A NEW SCHOOL
OR NONE AT ALL

WE ARE TIRED OF
TAR-PAPER SHACKS

The signs were to be carried on the school grounds only. No one was to leave until the end of the regular day. There was to be no mischief that could serve as an excuse to call in the police. Mean-

* From an interview with John Stokes in *They Closed Their Schools*, Bob Smith (Chapel Hill: University of North Carolina Press, 1965), p. 39.

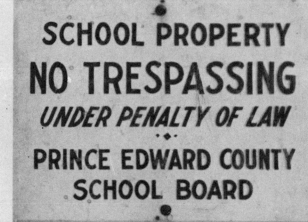

SCHOOL PROPERTY
NO TRESPASSING
UNDER PENALTY OF LAW
PRINCE EDWARD COUNTY
SCHOOL BOARD

Moton High School, Farmville, Virginia, shown during the period when the Prince Edward County Schools were closed.

while a delegation of student leaders would call on the superintendent of schools and present the strike demands.

The main demand was a new school or a remodeling job on Moton, which would amount to the same thing. Barbara Johns spoke of her own belief that "things would never be better until we had integration," * but that was not a demand. Integration was for the far-off future. Conditions at Moton were something to be changed right now. If the Moton students stayed on strike, the school board would have to make those changes, Barbara said. And if not, the NAACP had lawyers who could help the students file a lawsuit demanding their rights.

Twenty-four hours later the Prince Edward County student strike was news all over the state. The question most often heard in the white community was, "Who put them up to it?"

Actually no one had. Conditions at Moton, the contrast with conditions at the white high school, and the black students' pride—these were the triggers of action. But those who wanted "someone" to blame found several candidates. First, there was Principal Boyd Jones.

In one sense, he was responsible. For, as Barbara Johns said later, "his teaching made it inevitable." He had not only taught his students to have convictions and fight for them, but also had given them responsibility for running programs in the school to build their self-confidence and know-how. Jones was newly married and expecting a child, and needed his job at Moton. So the students had gone to great lengths not to involve him. That was why the mysterious caller had lured him away from the school. Unfortu-

* Ibid., p. 38.

nately, this sort of evidence did not convince Superintendent McIlwaine of Jones's "innocence," and at the end of the term, he was informed that he would not be rehired.

Another adult who was suspected of masterminding the strike was Barbara's uncle, Rev. Vernon Johns.* He was one of the earliest and most outspoken civil rights leaders of the South and had led many delegations in the 1940's to protest the lack of school buses in Prince Edward County. True, he was not even living in the state now, but it was said that Barbara spent many of her vacations at the Vernon Johns's home in Montgomery, Alabama.

Another adult who was blamed for the students' action was the local Baptist minister. Rev. Francis Griffin had grown up in Farmville, where his father was minister of the First Baptist Church, had gone away—first to war, then to college—and had come back in 1949 to take over his father's work. For two years he had been preaching, in the pulpit and out of it, that blacks would have to stand up and fight for their rights. He organized the Prince Edward County branch of the NAACP, and was on the P.T.A. delegation that kept pressing the school board. Rev. Griffin was the first adult called by the students after the strike assembly.

They called from the library of the school and asked him to come out and help settle a difference of opinion that had arisen. Some of the students wanted to go straight to the office of Superin-

---

* Rev. Johns was pastor of Montgomery, Alabama's, Dexter Avenue Baptist Church and began the agitation against that city's Jim Crow seating on city bus lines. He was actually arrested for refusing to move to the "colored" section several years before Mrs. Rosa Parks did the same thing and triggered the successful Montgomery bus boycott. Rev. Johns was succeeded in his pastorate by a young minister who was considered less militant—the eventual leader of the boycott movement, Dr. Martin Luther King, Jr.

[8]

tendent McIlwaine to present the strike demands before the general enthusiasm had a chance to cool. Others wanted to wait till they could talk to their parents. Rev. Griffin listened to both sides and made a simple suggestion: take a vote.

A vote was taken, and the majority was for going ahead without consulting anyone. So another phone call was made from the library, this one to Superintendent McIlwaine. But he had heard about the strike and refused to meet with any students until all were back in class.

At that point a third call was made. To Richmond. To the office of the NAACP. Someone there put the students in touch with an attorney named Oliver Hill. His firm, it turned out, was already handling a case involving the black schools of another south Virginia county.

Hill listened sympathetically to the students' complaint, but he too advised them to go back to class. He and his partner, Spottswood Robinson III, would be driving down to Pulaski County in a couple of days, and they would be glad to stop off, size up the situation, and see in what way they might be of help. But meanwhile, the strike should be called off.

The committee was discouraged. It seemed as if nothing they could do would make the adult world pay attention. But they kept their self-doubts to themselves and went ahead with the call on the superintendent of schools.

Carrying their placards, the little group marched bravely and silently through the streets of Farmville, past clumps of curious but equally silent whites, all the way to the courthouse; once there, they marched up its outside steps, up its inside stairs, to the office of Superintendent McIlwaine, who had said he wouldn't see them.

He did see them, finally, but very little was accomplished by the meeting, except to give the students more confidence. McIlwaine accused them of being "duped" by some adult agitator, refused to answer their questions, and threatened them with expulsion if they refused to call off the strike. But he impressed them as "timid and evasive." They left his office more determined than ever.

Early Wednesday morning there was a gathering of nearly two hundred people in the basement of Rev. Griffin's church. Many of the striking students were there and a good number of parents. The two lawyers from Richmond arrived, as they had promised they would.

Both Robinson and Hill knew something about the situation at Moton and their sympathies were on the side of the students. But the place for such a protest, they believed, was in the courts. Already there were a number of lawsuits involving black schools, one of which would surely be carried up to the U.S. Supreme Court. It was there that the issue would have to be settled in the end.

One such case was ready for trial in South Carolina. Another was on the court calendar in Kansas. Another was underway in the District of Columbia. And Virginia would not lag behind. The case that was taking the attorneys down to Pulaski County was a challenge to Virginia's school segregation law.

All this news about struggles outside their own region didn't persuade Moton students that they ought to give up their strike. It just made them more anxious "to get a piece of the action." To the warning that they could be arrested for violating the school attendance law, they replied with Barbara's phrase: "The jails aren't big enough to hold all of us."

Robinson and Hill asked how the adult community felt. There were different answers from different parts of the audience. Most of the parents were in sympathy with the students' demands, and some were willing to support the strike. Others felt it was the

Spottswood W. Robinson III (right) of Virginia, shown discussing a school integration case with Harold R. Boulware (left) of South Carolina and Thurgood Marshall of New York.

wrong way to go about things. Some—perhaps the majority—stood somewhere in between, wavering, open to persuasion.

The attorneys then asked another, more crucial question: How would the adult black community feel about a demand not for better schools, but for an end to segregated schools? Because that was the sort of school case the NAACP was interested in taking at this time.

There was instant agreement from the young people. Some had already thought about such a demand. Barbara had mentioned it in her Monday speech. Although that was only two days ago, already the idea seemed much less radical. After all, why not?

But there was uneasy silence from most of the adults. The lawyers noticed, but made no comment. They asked the students to think about the questions they had raised and talk to people who had not been present. If 95 percent of the parents of the striking students would back them in a demand for desegregation, rather than equalization of the schools in Prince Edward County, the law firm of Hill, Martin, and Robinson and the NAACP were willing to bring suit on their behalf.

A mass meeting had already been called for the following night —Thursday, April 26. Robinson and Hill would be in Pulaski County, but they promised to have W. Lester Banks, state secretary of the NAACP come to Farmville. The issue could be debated, questions asked and answered, and a final decision reached at that time.

Two dozen Moton students began going door to door with petitions, asking for signatures of parents willing to support a desegregation suit. It took a lot of talking, for black adults of Prince Edward County knew the minds of white people there better than the students did. While they might agree that "separate but equal" was never really equal, they knew that white resistance to desegregation would be bitter and stubborn, that those who provoked it would have to suffer the consequences. Many of them doubted that poor black farmers in a "poverty pocket" were the sort of citizens who ought to lead such a challenge.

Even so, the students did their work so well that by Thursday evening they had the signatures of a majority of their parents. Not 95 percent, but a majority all the same. And there were still many who had not yet made up their minds.

The mass meeting was held in the high school auditorium where the strike had begun on Monday. It was jammed to overflowing. Newspaper reporters were taking notes and pictures. Lester Banks explained the NAACP's position, why it was only interested in desegregation cases. Experience, he said, had proved that no black school, however fine and expensive, could ever offer its students an equal educational opportunity. People who disagreed with this spoke from the floor, but they were outnumbered by those who agreed. It was the sense of the meeting that the NAACP and its attorneys should take the Prince Edward County case to court as a desegregation suit.

Thirty Moton students agreed to put their names on a formal petition addressed to the Farmville School Board, asking it to admit black students to Farmville High School. This petition was to be delivered on Thursday, May 3. The board would be given five days in which to reply. Then, unless it had agreed (which was all but impossible), on Tuesday, May 8, the attorneys would file suit in federal court, asking an injunction to stop the school board from continuing its policy of separating students along racial lines.*

* On April 30, Robinson and Hill filed the same sort of suit in Pulaski County, but before it came to trial, the plaintiff died and the suit had to be dropped.

[13]

A second mass meeting was called for the evening of May 3. It was held in the main auditorium of the First Baptist Church, and drew another overflow crowd. There were a number of speakers, including Barbara Johns. She told the story of the past ten days from the viewpoint of the students. The applause at the end of Barbara's speech seemed to be unanimous.

But as it quieted, an opposing voice was heard.

It belonged to J. B. Pervall, who had once been principal of Moton High School. He had been against the strike from the beginning, but he had not spoken publicly till now.

"You are pulling a heavy load," he said, addressing himself to one of the lawyers, "coming down to a country town like Farmville and trying to take it over on a nonsegregated basis."

There was silence, and then a stirring and murmuring in the audience. Old fears, only just laid to rest, were wakened by his words. Perhaps it would be better to let some other community lead this fight after all . . . . Perhaps the demand should have been only improvement . . . equalization . . . .

But the question had been settled at the mass meeting of April 26. Legal action had already been taken. The formal petition, signed by thirty students, had been presented to the school board. To back down, or to change the demands now, would be taken as a sign of weakness or disunity.

The mood of solidarity and confidence was already dimming. No one seemed sure whether or how to answer Mr. Pervall. The silence grew uncomfortable. Then Barbara Johns came back to the speaker's stand.

"We are depending on you," she told the adults. She looked so young and so brave and so passionately in earnest that people felt tears rising in their eyes, as she appealed to the pride of the community in its children, and to its loyalty to them. Finally she touched on the spring of anger: "Don't let Mr. Charley, or Mr. Tommy, or Mr. Pervall stop you from backing us now!"

By "Mr. Tommy" she meant "Uncle Tom"—a term used by black people to describe other blacks who submit to the system that makes second-class citizens of them. The word did its work. Mr. Pervall lost his hold on the meeting and was not heard from again.

On Monday, May 7, the students of Moton High School returned to their classes.

They had done something that would stand as an example for other students to follow in the future, if and when the need should arise. The battle they had started by striking was now being carried to other grounds. It would be fought by others—by lawyers and judges and scholars and politicians. It would be long and costly and sometimes confusing. The students of Prince Edward County and their parents, and the teachers and preachers who had stood with them, would be called on for patience and courage and many sorts of sacrifice. But the action would take place too far away for them to be part of it.

On May 23, Spottswood Robinson and Oliver Hill—acting on behalf of thirty students of Moton High School—filed suit in federal court in Richmond, asking for the immediate integration of Prince Edward County's schools. Then they got into a car and started the drive south, to Charleston, where Robinson was to act as assistant counsel in the trial of the Clarendon County school desegregation case.

Clarendon County

The South Carolina case did not begin as a protest against segregation. It began—in November 1949—as a protest against the conditions of the schools in which the black children of Summerton were educated. As in Prince Edward County, it was a case of people finally getting fed up with humiliating, unequal, substandard schools. The difference was that in Clarendon County it was the parents, not the students, who finally took action.*

Also, the conditions in Clarendon County were worse. Three schools were involved: two elementary schools, and one which combined both elementary and high school. None had an indoor flush toilet. In one school, 694 pupils had to use one or the other of two, wooden-seated privies that stood over a hole dug in the earth. The white schools of the county were not luxurious, but they did have modern plumbing and enough toilets to meet state standards.

The white schools had drinking fountains; the black students had to carry water in in buckets. Many black schoolrooms had no desks. In Ram Bay Elementary School students did their lessons on two long, cracked tables. In another they had to write on their laps.

Two teachers taught all the seven grades at Ram Bay. Four teachers taught eight grades at Liberty Hill, another black school. As one reporter summed it up, "[Clarendon County's black schools]

---

* Some reporters believe that high school students prodded their parents into the action, but even so, Clarendon County represents in many ways a reverse twist on the Prince Edward story.

are poorly equipped, crude, inadequate, unsanitary, and badly staffed." *

In late 1949 a group of about one hundred parents had been organized by the NAACP to petition the school board of District 22 to "cease discrimination against Negro children of public school age." That took courage in a section where eighty years before, "white supremacy" had been reestablished by a campaign of organized terror against blacks. Black leaders braced themselves for another such backlash, and in due time it came—though not with the violence of the Redeemer movement of post-Reconstruction days.

There were threats of bombings; then bombings, both of homes and churches. Banks foreclosed loans to blacks. People lost jobs, and knew the reason. There was even a rumor that an unsolved murder in the county was connected with the school protest. This charge was never proved, but the rumor showed how much fear was loose in the community. Nevertheless, the petition was not withdrawn and finally the school board responded to it.

Some drinking fountains were installed at Scott's Branch Union School!

When the parents were convinced that the school board was going to stop there, they turned to the courts for help. Their lawyers filed a petition, asking a court order to bring about equality between the black and white school systems of the county. Just how unequal they were was illustrated by some official figures, which showed that although there were three times as many black students as

* *Richmond Afro-American,* June 2, 1951, p. 2.

whites in District 22, the black schools were valued at one-sixth the value of the white ones.*

The suit asked that this disproportion be ended, but the plaintiffs would probably have accepted any reasonable compromise. By the time the suit came to trial, many months later, something new had been added to the total picture, and an "amended complaint" changed the demand of the plaintiffs to one that could not be compromised.

That something new was contained in two opinions handed down by the U.S. Supreme Court in cases usually known by the names of the plaintiff in each of them: Herman Marion Sweatt of Texas in one; and G. W. McLaurin of Oklahoma in the other.

* *Richmond News-Leader* editorial, May 29, 1951, gave a similar set of figures: 73 percent of the pupils (black) had 13 percent of the school property (valued in dollars), while 27 percent (white) had 87 percent.

The Sweatt and
McLaurin Cases

Herman Marion Sweatt was a black student who had applied for admission to the University of Texas law school and been refused on account of his race. After a long delay and many hearings, Sweatt was finally notified by the university that he could study law in a special school set up for him in the basement of a building near the capitol grounds in Austin, while the state of Texas hurriedly built a two-million-dollar law school for blacks. Sweatt refused to attend the temporary school, and his lawyers appealed to the U.S. Supreme Court.

McLaurin was also a prospective law student. He finally managed to get himself admitted to the University of Oklahoma, but in accordance with the state's segregation law, he was required to sit at a special desk in the library, eat at a special table in the cafeteria, and listen to lectures at a desk placed in the anteroom of the hall in which white students were assembled.

Sweatt's lawyers argued that he could not get an equal education in a makeshift school, that he had a right to an equal education at once, not when the state of Texas got ready to give it to him on segregationist terms. McLaurin's position was different. He was in the same school, studying under the same professors, reading the same books as white students. But he testified that this "quite strange and humiliating position hinders me from doing effective work. I can't study and concentrate."

His lawyers argued that segregation itself was a denial of his rights under the U.S. Constitution—especially of its Fourteenth Amendment, passed after the Civil War to settle the status of

G. W. McLaurin sitting in an anteroom outside a classroom at the University of Oklahoma.

emancipated slaves. The "separate but equal" doctrine that made segregation legal was established twenty-eight years after the passage of the Fourteenth Amendment by the Supreme Court's decision in a famous case known as *Plessy* v. *Ferguson*. That case concerned the right of a Negro passenger to be served on a railroad dining car, and the Court decided that separating the races was not only legal, but also actually beneficial to both, so long as the facilities and opportunities offered black and white citizens were "substantially equal."

The Sweatt and McLaurin cases were considered so important that the attorneys general of most of the seventeen states that practiced de jure segregation (that is, segregation by law) wanted to take part. They appeared as amici curiae ("friends of the Court"), and asked that the justices take care "not to strike down their power to keep peace, order, and support their public schools" by overturning the "separate but equal" doctrine. The solicitor general of the United States also appeared as a "friend of the Court," but on the opposite side. His brief * stated that "the government submits that the . . . assumptions upon which *Plessy* v. *Ferguson* was decided have been demonstrated to be erroneous, . . . [T]he phrase 'equal rights' means the same rights."

Chief Justice Fred Vinson wrote the Supreme Court's opinion in both the Sweatt and McLaurin cases, which were decided on the same day in June 1950. He said nothing about *Plessy* v. *Ferguson* or "separate but equal." Instead, he considered the question raised by Sweatt's lawyers: whether or not he could get an equal education in a one-man, temporary law school. In Vinson's opinion, the answer was no. And he went a step further. As someone

---

* A brief is a legal argument, not necessarily brief at all.

who knew a thing or two about the law schools, he said that no "special"—that is, black-only—law school could ever give its students what they could get in the law department of the University of Texas. It was not just a matter of buildings and books and professors, he said. There were other things—such as tradition and prestige, such as the opportunity to make contacts that would help a young lawyer get a job after graduation. The only way to give Sweatt an equal opportunity to enjoy all these things was to admit him into the university's law department.

In the Oklahoma case, Vinson's opinion went farther still. He agreed with McLaurin that the treatment he was getting was bound to "impair and inhibit his ability . . . to learn his profession." And since a lawyer's professional training had a lot to do with how well he would serve his clients in the future, not only the lawyer but also those future clients had rights that had to be protected. The only way to do that was to give McLaurin an equal chance at the best available professional training, in the institutions set up for that purpose by his state.

When people studied the Vinson opinions, they saw that the logic could be applied to other professions besides law. For instance, medicine. What about the rights of medical students—future doctors and their future patients? Could a university's medical school refuse admission to black applicants under this view of the Constitution? And what about the teaching profession? If the training of a teacher was bound to affect his ability to serve his future students, how could any black applicant be denied admission to any college or university?

All this meant that segregation was being declared unconstitutional not just in graduate and professional schools, but in all the colleges and universities of the South!

In the months that followed, graduate schools, law schools,

medical schools, and even some colleges (everywhere in the country except in the "hard-core" states of Alabama, South Carolina, Florida, Georgia, and Mississippi) began to admit black students. Some did so voluntarily. Others resisted until a court case was threatened.

Southern politicians and newspaper editors began to argue over just where the "line of no retreat" was going to be drawn. Maybe it would be necessary to admit blacks to colleges and universities that were supported by the public's tax money. But public high schools and elementary schools were another matter. People who defined the "southern way of life" in terms of separation between black and white seemed to agree that segregation must be maintained in the first twelve grades at any cost.

Just what "any cost" might amount to became clear when there began to be discussion about closing down the public school system in some areas rather than "permit the intimate mingling of white and colored boys and girls during the formative years of adolescence." * The fear that lay behind that threat was seldom put into words, but all southerners—black and white—knew what it was. It was that letting down the barriers between children of the two races would eventually lead to mixed marriages, or what segregationists sometimes called "the mongrelization" of the white race.

Within a few days of the Sweatt and McLaurin decisions, the lawyers who had carried the cases to the U.S. Supreme Court met to discuss what their next moves should be.

Most of them were on the legal staff of the NAACP, which had been campaigning for twenty years to win improvements in

* *Richmond News-Leader*, May 7, 1951.

[23]

black education without risking a head-on collision with the "separate but equal" doctrine. The question was whether they should go on doing the same thing, or change to a new attack.

Should they use the threat of a possible Supreme Court "review" of *Plessy* v. *Ferguson* as a lever to pry more concessions out of white school boards? Things like better buildings in Summerton and Farmville? more and better school buses? salary raises to bring black teachers up to a par with whites? Or should they take aim at segregation itself?

There were risks in the latter course.

For one thing, if desegregation suits were brought and won, there would be real resistance against enforcing the new order of things. If angry whites were to close down public schools rather than admit black children to all-white ones, it was the black children who stood to suffer most. For white parents could find ways to operate "private" schools, with or without help from tax monies. Black parents couldn't. Black children might have to go without schooling of any kind, at least for some time.*

Also there would be violence. And violence of this kind was almost always directed against blacks. It was they who would be hurt, burned, bombed, possibly killed.

On the other hand, if desegregation suits were brought and lost, it might mean the end of all concessions granted to blacks. If—as some people believed—all the gains of the past twenty years had been "handouts" from Mr. Charley to keep Uncle Tom content and quiet, then any rebellion by southern blacks was sure to be punished.

---

* In Prince Edward County the public schools were actually closed for four years.

[24]

Nevertheless, after discussion and a two-day conference between lawyers and delegates from NAACP branches in twenty-two states, Thurgood Marshall, special counsel of the organization, announced to the press on June 28, 1950, that the NAACP was going to "insist on nonsegregation in American public education . . . from law school to kindergarten."

There were three kinds of reasons for the decision. First, most civil rights leaders were convinced that equality in education was impossible so long as it had to be segregated. Two separate systems were too expensive to equalize. The U.S. Office of Education estimated that to bring the black schools of the South up to parity with the white schools would cost about two billion dollars. That was more than the South, or the nation, was willing to spend.

Second, black people had long believed, and social scientists could now prove, that segregation itself kept black students from learning. Despite the fine words in the *Plessy* opinion about segregation not "necessarily imply[ing] the inferiority of either race to the other," black students knew they were considered "unfit to associate with others of different color." * In other words, they were inferior. And if they were inferior, why fight it? So they tended to become discouraged more easily than white children, to drop out of school at an early age. It seemed foolish to fight for better black schools if black children's ability to learn was being stunted in those schools just because they were "all black."

Finally, there was the consideration of timing. Sooner or later it was going to be necessary to attack *Plessy* v. *Ferguson* if black Americans were ever going to achieve first-class citizenship, and it

* From Judge Waites Waring's dissenting opinion in *Briggs* v. *Elliott*.

[25]

seemed that the time was ripe now. There had been a series of Supreme Court decisions, beginning in 1935, which seemed to point to an overturning of the "separate but equal" theory. The government's own official lawyer had called for it. (See p. 21.) It might take a few more cases, a few more failures, but if final victory was in sight, this was the time to keep the pressure up, not let it down.

All these reasons were presented and discussed at the national convention of the NAACP, which followed the June conference, and the new attack was officially accepted. State and local branches in seventeen southern and border states that practiced segregation began to discuss bringing suits in their own regions. Plaintiffs were needed—parents of elementary or high school students willing to challenge the laws that relied on *Plessy* v. *Ferguson*.

It was expected that the test cases would be brought in some of the larger cities where the black community was fairly well-organized and prosperous, able to protect itself and to carry the costs of a long court battle. But instead the first case came from the poorest of people in the most isolated part of the "hard-core" state of South Carolina.

Briggs v. *Elliott*

In November 1950, *The New York Times* carried a short news item which said that Judge Waites Waring of Charleston, South Carolina, had told representatives of the NAACP that if they would bring a desegregation suit in his district, he would call a three-judge federal court to rule on the constitutionality of the state's school segregation law.

A few weeks later, sixty-six of the original plaintiffs in Clarendon County changed their complaint and asked instead "the immediate granting of their rights under the Fourteenth Amendment to the U.S. Constitution in the matter of segregation in education." The suit was filed as *Briggs* v. *Elliott*, Mr. Briggs being one of the parent-plaintiffs, and Mr. Elliott, chairman of the Board of Trustees of School District 22.

The school board replied—not very promptly—denying that there was any discrimination against black students in the district. It had "investigated the complaint" and found that "the facilities and opportunities furnished to the colored children are substantially the same as those provided to the whites." * No comment was made on the question of the "equal protection of the law," required by the Fourteenth Amendment.

Briggs v. *Elliott* was set for trial in Charleston on May 28, 1951. The three-judge panel was headed by Circuit Judge John J. Parker, assisted by District Judges George Bell Timmerman and J. Waites Waring. National attention was focused on the trial, not

---

* From Judge Waring's dissenting opinion, quoting from the answer to the amended complaint.

only because it was the first of the desegregation suits, but also because of the personalities involved.

Heading the staff of attorneys for the plaintiffs (the black parents of Clarendon County) was Thurgood Marshall, who had argued the Sweatt case before the U.S. Supreme Court and had become the leading legal spokesman of the NAACP's integration effort. Marshall was a tall, handsome man, intelligent, courageous, dramatic in manner—the sort of champion behind whom humble but determined citizens could rally.* Assisting him were five other black attorneys from South Carolina, New York, Virginia, Georgia, and Alabama. These were lieutenants who would become captains in other battles as the campaign developed.

On the opposing side, besides the defense attorney for the school board of District 22, there were several distinguished "observers," who took no active part but whose very presence made news. One was the attorney general of South Carolina; another was the assistant attorney general of Virginia.

On the bench was perhaps the most controversial figure in the judicial profession of that day: Judge J. Waites Waring, a white, Charleston-born aristocrat, who had shocked the whole South a few years before by ruling that the "lily-white primary" was unconstitutional and could not be enforced. For the "sin" of forcing the Democratic party to permit black citizens to vote in its primary election, Waring and his wife were boycotted by Charleston's white society. Garbage was dumped on their doorstep, and bricks were hurled through the windows of their parlor. They were still, in

---

* Thurgood Marshall was to become in the 1960's the first black solicitor general of the U.S. and later the first black associate justice of the U.S. Supreme Court.

1951, threatened by anonymous phone calls at odd hours of the day and night.

Under these circumstances, it was not surprising that reporters from all over the nation came to Charleston to cover the opening of the Clarendon County case. What was surprising was how many black people—from Charleston, from the countryside around it, and from back-country districts like the home of the plaintiffs—crowded into the city to be witnesses of the trial.

By seven o'clock in the morning of a hot, humid day, people began filing into the post-office building where the courtroom was located on an upper floor. By eight o'clock there was a milling crowd in the corridors. Only a few of those who got inside the building got seats in the courtroom, but the rear doors of that chamber were left open, and a quiet, densely packed crowd stood, hour after hour, straining their eyes and ears to catch what was being said inside.

What the crowd heard that first day was also surprising. The defense began by admitting what it had previously denied: that there were inequalities between the black and white schools of District 22. The defendants' attorney explained that they "had not intended to discriminate" and that given time and some hoped-for money from the state, they would "act in good faith to formulate a plan for ending such inequalities." *

This caught Marshall and the other NAACP lawyers off guard. They had planned to call many witnesses that morning to prove that there were inequalities. Witnesses they intended to call about other points had not been asked to be in Charleston until the second

* From Judge Waring's summary of the case in his dissent.

[29]

day of the trial. Now hurried long-distance calls had to be made. Airplane flights arranged. Schedules changed.

But after some confusion and delay, the plaintiffs' lawyer called the first of a series of "experts" to the witness stand. These experts were scientists and educators, professors of psychology, sociology, and political science. There were men and women on the list, holding many degrees and posts of honor at such institutions as Columbia, Harvard, and Yale universities, Vassar College, the City College of New York, Howard University, West Virginia Wesleyan, and the universities of Chicago, Michigan, California, and Louisville. They had come to Charleston to tell the court what they knew about the effect of racial segregation on school children, both black and white.

Each of them spoke from the viewpoint of the particular field in which he or she was trained. But what each said supported the conclusion that separation of races in a democratic society cannot exist without discrimination against one race and harm to both.

One psychologist said that white children suffered because they were confused about basic moral values when "the same people who talk ... about love and brotherhood also teach [them] to segregate." But the effects on black children were of course far worse. One of the other psychologists said, "Segregation does not prepare children to be members of the human race."

Another, a visiting professor at Harvard, startled the courtroom by remarking that "the Negro is inferior because the white has made him so." Where segregated black schools are also inferior, as was admittedly the case in Clarendon County, "black children were apt to develop ... a lower ability to cope with life."

Thurgood Marshall put it a different way when he said in his final summary: "All your state officials are white. All your school officials are white. That's not just segregation. It's exclusion from the group that runs everything. The Negro child is made to go to an inferior school; he is branded in his own mind as inferior. This sets up a road block in his mind. . . . There is no relief for the Negro children . . . except to be permitted to attend existing and superior white schools."

Marshall ridiculed the defense's request for more time to correct inequalities. "I know of no statute that permits anyone to come into court and ask time to stop doing something unlawful. . . ." And Clarendon County was "violating the law every day it operates this school system," he said.

Finally, he attacked South Carolina's state law requiring the separation of races in schools. Article II, Section 7, of the state constitution, which was rewritten in 1895, took back from the state's black citizens most of the rights granted them in the constitution of 1868. The question Marshall was asking about this change in 1951 was the same that black Congressman Robert Smalls had asked then: Can South Carolina or any other state legislate out of existence those words in the U.S. Constitution that guarantee to citizens of the nation "equal protection under the law"?

The court seemed impressed by Marshall's argument. But as Judge Parker noted, what was being asked of the court was something the U.S. Supreme Court had not yet been willing to do—to overturn the *Plessy* v. *Ferguson* precedent. It was a serious step for a lower court and must be carefully considered. Judge Parker asked the attorneys for both sides to submit written arguments on the constitutional question. Time would be granted for the preparation and study of such briefs.

Meanwhile, the court took the case of *Briggs* v. *Elliott* "under advisement," and adjourned with no certain date set for the handing down of a decision.

But the decision came sooner than expected.

On June 24, 1951, not quite a month later, it was announced: two to one in favor of the defendants. Judges Parker and Timmerman did not find that segregation in the schools of Clarendon County violated any citizens' rights. They gave the school board six months to come up with a plan for improving the black schools, but they refused to order the admission of black children into the white schools while those improvements were being made.

Judge Waring dissented. He said that testimony given in the trial "showed beyond a doubt that segregation . . . is an evil that must be eradicated.

"And if the courts of this land are to render justice . . . for all men and all kinds of men, the time to do it is now, and the place is in the elementary schools where our future citizens learn their first lesson to respect the individual in a democracy."

As the NAACP lawyers began to prepare their appeal to the U.S. Supreme Court, one sentence of Judge Waring's dissent stood like a title to their argument:

"Segregation," he had written, "is inequality."

Brown v.
Board of Education
of Topeka

The day after the court in Charleston decided *Briggs* v. *Elliott,* a court in Kansas began to hear another school segregation case. This one also had begun as an equalization case, a protest by black parents against the fact that their children were required to attend inferior schools. But this one was different from both the Prince Edward and Clarendon County protests in several important ways.

For one, Topeka was not a small country town. It was the capital of the state. And Kansas was not a part of the old Confederacy. It had been "free" since the days of John Brown. Segregation was not required by its constitution. It was *permitted* in cities of 15,000 or more that voted for it. Some Kansas cities had laws separating the races not only in schools, but also in other forms of public accommodation. Others didn't. In Topeka, the high schools were more or less integrated by the mid 1940's, but the elementary schools were not.

Another unique aspect of the Topeka situation was that there was no great difference between white and black schools. Many black parents didn't even know that their children were missing some of the advantages offered to whites, as for example school music programs, with an orchestra or band. They were reasonably well satisfied with the kind of education their children were getting. What bothered them was transportation. Bussing!

There were only four elementary schools for blacks in Topeka, one in each quarter of the city. If a black family lived far from one of these, their child had to be bused (or driven in the family car), and very often right past a white school to which the child could have walked. Sometimes this worked out so that the child had to wait for as much as an hour, in whatever the weather might be, for the school doors to open in the morning, or the bus to pick him or her up on the return trip.

Annoying as this was, it might not have sparked anything as serious as a lawsuit if something else had not stung the black community into action. What did that was the hiring of a new director of black schools, who set to work on a program of change that many parents saw as "*re*segregation." Herman Caldwell, a black man himself, was held responsible for what happened not only in the four black elementary schools, but for what happened to black students in the integrated high school as well.

For instance, Caldwell inaugurated a system of two bells for assemblies. The first called white students to the auditorium. The second, known as "the nigger bell," called black students to an upstairs classroom where they had to listen to a talk by Caldwell, or perhaps watch some slides. Caldwell also isolated the black athletes and set up a Jim Crow schedule for them with all-black teams from out of town. Black girl students were no longer included in the regular domestic science classes, but were farmed out as unpaid mother's helpers in the homes of black housewives. And once, at Caldwell's order, black students were turned away from the door at the senior prom, directed to another address where there was to be a "special party" for them alone.

"He woke some of us up to what a horrible thing segregation was," one of the parents has said. "We'd been living with it so

The Buchanan (black) School in Topeka, Kansas.

long it had become almost a way of life. But when Mr. Caldwell began tearing down any little gains we'd made over the years, that started us to thinking. When we wanted to get rid of him, we found we had to get rid of segregation itself. Because that was what he was put in office for—to keep other blacks in their places!"

Mrs. Lucinda Todd, who was one of the first parents to clash with Caldwell, was a member of the Topeka branch of the NAACP, a small group of middle-class citizens, that had been organized some years before by a local attorney, Elisha Scott. Scott was a real pioneer in the civil rights field. He had won a number of desegregation suits in the 1940's and argued one of them before the U.S. Supreme Court at a time when that was almost unheard of for a black. But by 1950 he was in poor health and had retired from active life. A new chairman had taken over the branch, and two of Scott's sons—John and Charles—had graduated from law school and had come back to Topeka to practice.

It was this little group that now began the drive to unseat Caldwell and reverse the trend toward resegregation. They began by writing to the national NAACP office for advice. The suggestion they got was to collect signatures on a petition asking for an end to segregated schools in Topeka. If 1,000 signatures could be gathered from the 10,000 black families of the city, the school board would have to take the matter seriously.

Such a petition was drawn up, and the job of carrying it door to door in the black community began. It was hard and sometimes dangerous work. As soon as news of it reached the white Establishment, Caldwell began visiting the employers of men who were involved in the campaign (usually through their wives' activities). Black teachers were warned that integration, if it came, would cost

The Gage (white) School in Topeka, Kansas.

[37]

them their jobs. Contracts were held up in the cases of teachers suspected of belonging to the NAACP.

"We were treated as crackpots and radicals," says Mrs. Todd. "Friendships of long standing were destroyed. . . . We never could have done it without help. But we got it; partly from the national NAACP; partly from the Menninger people.* Both the doctors Menninger were wonderful to us, and the young graduates who were working at the clinic helped carry our petitions around. Sometimes, when we needed to, we even met at homes out there—though the people who let us had their phones bugged as a result. And there were other folks who helped in places like Kansas City and other parts of the state.

"In the end we had almost 1,500 signatures! That was really something! So many Negro taxpayers willing to stand up and say that they didn't want segregated schools anymore!"

The petition and the signatures were presented first to the school board, which took no action, then to the New York office of the NAACP, which agreed to help in the filing of a suit.

"But for that we had to have plaintiffs," says Mrs. Todd, "and finding them was another big job."

Mrs. Todd was one of the first to put her name down. She and Mr. Todd had a daughter, Nancy, in the fourth grade. Since Alvin Todd's employer was the federal government, he felt reasonably secure, although Caldwell did go out and talk to his boss. But other fathers were not so well situated. Even an independent businessman could be made to feel pressure. The one profession that was almost immune was the ministry. So an effort was made to find a

---

* The Menninger Foundation maintains a large mental hospital and clinic on the outskirts of Topeka.

"man of the cloth" who had a child in the public schools and a grievance against the status quo.

Someone finally approached Rev. Oliver Brown.

He was not a member of the NAACP nor active in any other civil rights effort, but his little daughter, Linda, had a particularly bad bussing problem. The Browns agreed to join the suit. Slowly other names were added until there were thirteen in all. When the Kansas names were listed alphabetically, Brown came first. Thus it happened that the name of a plaintiff who was not one of the leaders in the desegregation effort came to be used as the "title"—first in the Topeka case, and later in the group of five cases that were consolidated by the U.S. Supreme Court.*

The local lawyers were joined by two from the New York NAACP staff,** one of whom had taken part in the South Carolina trial. They worked out a courtroom strategy by which they hoped to sharpen the basic issue, as they saw it. In the *Briggs* case, the plaintiffs had set out to prove two things: first, that black and white schools were not equal; and second, that it was a denial of the children's constitutional rights to segregate them at all.

On the first point, they had won. The defense had granted the point before they had a chance to argue it. But the second point, on which they had lost, was the important one. The new strategy was a reverse twist on the tactic of the Clarendon County defense: the

---

* There seems to be no reason for the *Brown* case being listed first by the U.S. Supreme Court, as it was neither the first of the cases to be tried, or appealed, nor the first alphabetically.

** Topekans Charles Bledsoe and John and Charles Scott were joined by Robert Carter and Jack Greenberg of New York. Carter had been an associate counsel in Charleston and Greenberg would appear later in the Delaware case.

[39]

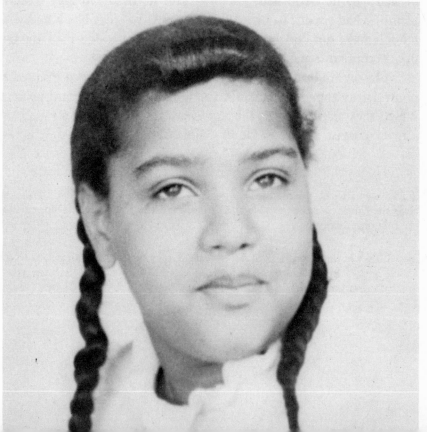

Topeka plaintiffs would admit (for the sake of argument) that there was no inequality between the black and white schools involved. The court's decision would thus have to be rendered on the simple, basic issue of segregation: what harm it did the children who were subjected to it, and what rights were violated by imposing it.

As in *Briggs* v. *Elliott*, experts were called to the stand to testify about the psychological and educational effects of the system as it was practiced in Topeka. For the first time in such a trial, one of the children who were the subject of the whole struggle took the witness stand. Little Katherine Carper, a fourth-grade pupil, testified about her experience—particularly the bussing part of it. But perhaps the deepest impression was made by Silas Fleming, the father of two boys.

Fleming asked to be allowed to explain why he had "joined the suit, whole soul and body." Permission was granted, and he said, "Not only I and my children are craving light. The entire colored race is craving light. And the only way to reach the light is to start our children together in their infancy and they come up together."

The verdict of the court was against Mr. Fleming and the other parents, but only because the judges felt that the U.S. Supreme Court must take responsibility for overturning as old a precedent as *Plessy* v. *Ferguson*. The feeling of the three Kansas judges, as expressed by Judge Walter Huxman, was that segregation was wrong because:

"Segregation with the sanction of the law . . . has a tendency to retard the educational and mental development of Negro children and to deprive them of some of the benefits they would receive in a racially integrated school system."

Above, Mrs. Lucinda Todd with a portrait of her daughter Nancy, done at the time of the Brown case. Below, Katherine Carper of Topeka, Kansas.

The Other
School Cases

The Prince Edward County case was tried under the title *Davis* v. *County School Board,* and the verdict was the same as that in *Briggs* v. *Elliott.* Again, expert witnesses testified about the effects of segregation, and this time they appeared for each of the opposing sides.

The chief witness for the defense (the Farmville School Board) was Dr. Henry E. Garrett of Columbia University. He began by saying that segregation was psychologically harmful to children who were forced by it to attend an inferior school. But the school board had promised to bring the black schools of Prince Edward County up to the level of the white schools, and construction was already going forward (by the time of the trial) on a new high school to replace Moton.

Assuming that the promise would be fulfilled, Dr. Garrett said it was possible that segregation might work to the benefit of both races. "I think, in the high schools of Virginia, if the Negro child has equal facilities, his own teachers, his own friends, and a good feeling, he would be more likely to develop pride in himself as a Negro . . . develop his own potentialities. . . . [T]he Negroes might develop their schools up to the level where . . . they would say, 'We prefer to remain as a Negro group.' In a mixed school . . . a great many animosities, disturbances, resentments and hostilities and inferiorities would develop. . . ."

Twenty years after Dr. Garrett's testimony there would be many Negro educators and political leaders who had reached the same conclusion, but for a different reason: that whites would never give black children a truly equal school opportunity. But in

1952 there was a hope that the end of racial separation in the public schools of the country would open the doors of full citizenship to all and begin a new era of democracy in the United States.

In October 1952, the U.S. Supreme Court agreed to hear the appeal from the Virginia decision along with the appeals it had already agreed to hear from South Carolina and Kansas. One month later another case was added to the list. Or, more exactly, a pair of cases, which had been tried in Wilmington, Delaware, under the titles *Bulah* v. *Gebhart* and *Belton* v. *Gebhart*.

Both involved black students in segregated schools: one, an elementary school in Hockessin, thirty miles northwest of Wilmington; the other, a high school—or the lack of one—in Claymont, a suburb north of the city. In both, the triggering problem was transportation. The state's segregation law made it necessary to bus black children for long distances, frequently in dangerously decrepit buses.

In the case of Shirley Bulah no bus was available. There was a school bus that passed the child's house, but she was not permitted to ride on it, for a court had ruled that a school bus was "an integral part of a school program"—a white school program, from which she was barred. The problem in Claymont was that there was no black high school closer than Wilmington, and that meant a two-hour trip every day for Ethel Belton and the other students whose parents brought the lawsuit.

Louis L. Redding, the Wilmington attorney who represented both sets of plaintiffs, decided to bring suit not in a federal, but in a state court. This was a new tactic, and in some ways a risky one. The decision of a state court could not be appealed directly to the U.S. Supreme Court, as could the decisions of the three-judge courts that had heard all the other school cases. That could mean an extra legal step that could—and surely would—mean more time and more

[43]

money. Also the judge who would hear the argument in a state court was more sensitive to prevailing public opinion than a federal judge, for he would have to run for reelection at the end of his term, while federal judges were appointed for "life or good behavior."

But Redding's decision and his handling of the case * resulted in the one favorable lower court decision of the whole desegregation effort. Chancellor Collins J. Seitz deferred (as the Kansas judges had before him) to the U.S. Supreme Court on the matter of overturning the *Plessy* v. *Ferguson* "separate but equal" doctrine. But he could and did find substantial inequality between Delaware's black and white schools. Unlike the Virginia and South Carolina judges he ruled that relief from it must be immediate. Black children must be admitted at once to the schools nearest their homes, schools that had been intended for white children only.

The state appealed to its state supreme court, which upheld Chancellor Seitz and refused to cancel the integration order. The state appealed again, this time to the U.S. Supreme Court. But by that time black children in at least two districts of the segregated South had begun attending school with whites. There was no outcry against this change in the "traditional southern way of life." No violence. No boycott.

At about the same time a fifth case was added to the list before the high Court. This one was brought on behalf of a boy who had applied for admission to a white junior high school in Washington, D.C. Spottswood Thomas Bolling's lawyers ** argued that the District of Columbia had no law that mentioned school segre-

---

* He was assisted by Jack Greenberg of the national NAACP staff.

** George E. C. Hayes and James M. Nabrit, Jr., then a professor of law at Howard University and later its president.

Spottswood Thomas Bolling (left) of Washington, D.C., the central figure in a segregation case in the nation's capital.

gation one way or the other. There was no reason to assume that Congress, which made the laws for the District, had intended to require segregation. To deny a student the freedom to enroll in the school of his choice was a violation of the Fifth Amendment, which says that no citizen shall be deprived of liberty or property "without due process of law."

The district court denied relief, and the U.S. Supreme Court let it be known that it was willing to hear the argument in *Bolling* v. *Sharpe* while it was considering the appeals in the four other school cases. So the United States Court of Appeals for the D.C. circuit passed it on up without hearing it. The combination of five cases, each representing a slightly different legal aspect of the whole problem, was scheduled for oral argument in December 1952.

Two
Supreme Court
Decisions

As the time for that argument approached, all sorts of historic events were getting front-page treatment in American newspapers. The United States was fighting a bloody, although undeclared, war in Korea. There was a national election in which the Republican presidential candidate defeated the Democratic candidate for the first time in twenty years. Dwight D. Eisenhower, the new president, flew to the battle zone of the Far East and began negotiations for a cease-fire.

But in the second week of December 1952, without headlines, history was being made in the softly lit, almost silent chambers of the U.S. Supreme Court in Washington. The nine justices, robed in black, sat in their high-backed chairs, behind the long table that serves as a "bench," and listened to the two sides of the most serious difference of opinion that would come before them in their professional lives.

Mountains of paper had been submitted to them for study. The attorney general of the United States had filed a brief giving the government's position. The attorneys general of four southern states and the District of Columbia had submitted official positions. And thirty-two of the country's leading educators and social scientists had submitted a document called *The Effects of Segregation and the Consequences of Desegregation*.

The oral arguments were made for the most part by Thurgood

Marshall, for the plaintiffs, and John W. Davis, for the defendants.* There was nothing particularly new in them, although both sides were presented eloquently and forcefully. Perhaps the most significant words were spoken almost casually by one of the judges—Robert Jackson **—who remarked that "the reason this case is here is that action couldn't be obtained from Congress." That was the heart of a difference within the Court which was to keep it deadlocked for almost three years.

For there were two schools of thought on whether or not the high Court ought to act in place of Congress to "make policy for the nation." Those who leaned to one side were called "judicial activists," and those on the other "believers in judicial restraint." Some of the men who were most sympathetic to the plaintiffs' view of their constitutional rights were also opposed to having the Court "make law," as for example Justice Hugo Black of Alabama.

It was hard to forecast how each man would resolve the contradiction between restraint and activism, and even harder to guess how each would vote on the constitutional question. Chief Justice Vinson, for example, was a conservative on most issues, but it was he who had written the Sweatt and McLaurin opinions, which opened the way for the desegregation suits. Justice Felix Frankfurter had served on the legal committee of the NAACP for ten years. Would that make him favor the NAACP's position now, or lean over backward to avoid seeming biased?

* Davis had the reputation of having won more Supreme Court cases than any other single man.

** Before his appointment to the Court, Jackson had been attorney general of the United States and had taken a leave from the Court to serve as prosecutor of German war criminals in the trials at Nuremberg after World War II.

[48]

From the day the arguments closed on December 11, 1952, there was suspense about the outcome. As January, February, March, and even April passed with no word from the Court, the suspense grew greater. The Court was due to adjourn for the summer in June. So there was an unusually large crowd in the chambers on June 8—the last day of the session—when the decision on *Brown* v. *Board of Education of Topeka* was finally announced.

The decision was—not to decide! At least not yet.

Instead, the Court had drawn up a list of questions to be answered by both sides and other interested parties. The answers were to be submitted in writing when the Court reconvened in the fall, at which time it would hear "further oral argument."

The first of the questions had to do with the meaning of the Fourteenth Amendment (see p. 19). Just what had its framers intended when they wrote, "No state shall make or enforce any law which shall abridge the privileges or amenities of citizens . . . nor deny to any person the equal protection of the law"? Was racial segregation an abridgment of a citizen's privileges and amenities? Was that what Congress understood when it passed the amendment in 1868? What about the state legislatures that ratified it? Did the statesmen of the post-Civil War era mean to abolish all forms of discrimination by federal statute, or was it understood that matters like education would be left to state and local authorities to decide?

The other questions on the list had to do with how much detail the Court should go into in working out whatever decision it finally reached.

All through the summer, historians and legal scholars combed through records, books, newspapers, commentaries, and papers—public and private. The research done by the plaintiffs' side made a book 235 pages long. And to no one's surprise, the answers presented to the Court were as opposite as the arguments on the issue

[49]

itself. One side found that the framers of the Fourteenth Amendment did mean it to apply to discrimination in education; the other, that they did not. One side found that the Supreme Court had the right—and the duty—to make specific rules and orders about applying its decision; the other, that it had no such rights, that *Plessy* v. *Ferguson* proved just that.

And this time a long list of organizations submitted briefs as "friends of the Court," most of them on the plaintiffs' side.* Public interest was at an all-time high.

The Court that heard the second round of arguments had a new chief justice, who added another element of suspense. Justice Vinson had died during the recess and had been replaced by Governor Earl Warren of California. No one had any idea how he would view this case.

He was a Republican. A westerner. He had never held any judicial office before. His record on the rights of minorities was not particularly good. He had been attorney general of California when the Japanese attacked Pearl Harbor at the start of World War II, and he bore some of the responsibility for the policy that herded 100,000 Japanese-Americans into concentration camps without "due process of law." On the other hand, as governor, he had done his part to protect the returning Japanese-Americans from vigilante violence when a decision of the U.S. Supreme Court released them from detention.

---

* Among the organizations were the American Civil Liberties Union, the American Federation of Teachers, the American Jewish Congress, the American Veterans Committee, the Catholic Interracial Council, the Friends Committee on National Legislation, the Japanese-American Citizens League, the Unitarian Fellowship for Social Justice, the Washington Federation of Churches, the Washington Bar Association, and the Congress of Industrial Unions, whose brief was signed by its general counsel, Arthur Goldberg.

Attorneys who argued the case against segregation stand together smiling in front of the U.S. Supreme Court Building. Left to right: George E. C. Hayes, Washington, D.C.; Thurgood Marshall, special counsel for the NAACP; and James M. Nabrit, Jr., professor of law at Howard University in Washington and later the university's president.

A crowd of people lined up in the Supreme Court Building in Washington, December 7, 1953, to enter the courtroom for the second round of arguments challenging the constitutionality of school segregation.

The second round of arguments was heard in December 1953. Again month after month went by with no sign of a decision. The issue had been before the courts of the country since early 1951, before the U.S. Supreme Court since late the same year. It seemed impossible that it could drag on any longer. But it was the middle of May 1954 before the suspense was broken.

On May 17, Chief Justice Warren read an opinion that he had written and to which there was unanimous agreement. All the other justices were present that Monday morning to make their agreement plain—even Justice Jackson, who was seriously ill and had to leave a hospital bed to be there.*

In language that he had been careful to make "short, understandable by the lay public, and unemotional," Warren answered the constitutional question that had been raised: "Separate educational facilities are inherently unequal . . . such segregation is a denial of the equal protection of the laws."

The reasons for this opinion were set forth in more detail, but still in language that citizens with no legal training could understand. "Education is perhaps the most important function of state and local governments. . . . [It] is required in the performance of our most basic public responsibilities. . . . It is the very foundation of good citizenship. . . . In these days it is doubtful that any child may reasonably be expected to succeed in life if he is denied the opportunity of an education. Such an opportunity . . . is a right which must be made available to all on equal terms."

And "any language in *Plessy* v. *Ferguson* contrary to this finding is rejected."

* Justice Jackson died during the year that followed and was replaced on the Court by John Marshall Harlan.

However, on the question of just how and when the corpse of Jim Crow was to be buried, the Court was postponing its final decision once again. It wanted more answers to its questions about details and timing. It had decided that the five cases were "class actions"—that is, they applied to all citizens in the same situation as the plaintiffs. That meant thousands of communities with different conditions and problems. How far should the Court go in making rules to apply to all? And how fast should it proceed? "Forthwith," or with enough time to permit a "gradual adjustment" to the new order of things?

This delayed final action for another whole year. During that time some states desegregated of their own volition. Others waited for the mandate of the Court. Some southern states had announced that they would obey that mandate when it came. South Carolina, Georgia, Mississippi, and Virginia were preparing to defy it.

When the high schools of Washington, D.C., admitted black students for the first time in the fall of 1954, white students struck and carried placards that read

GIVE US BACK
OUR SCHOOLS

NIGGERS GO BACK
TO AFRICA

But when local authorities acted firmly and promptly, this sort of resistance melted away. There was some reason to hope that a Supreme Court decision that decreed integration in all schools immediately would bring the long, agonizing controversy to an end.

But the conflict within the Court between the activists and the believers in judicial restraint was being decided the other way. The justices believed that their duty was not only to interpret the Con-

The Supreme Court that handed down the school segregation decision. Left to right, front row: Felix Frankfurter, Hugo L. Black, Chief Justice Earl Warren, Stanley F. Reed, and William O. Douglas. Back row: Tom C. Clark, Robert Jackson, Harold H. Burton, Sherman Minton.

stitution, but also to preserve the authority and prestige of the Court itself. As Justice Black put it, "Nothing is more important than that the Court do not decree what it cannot enforce." In view of the emotional fears of many white southerners, it seemed safer to proceed with what Justice Frankfurter called "all deliberate speed."

And so, on May 31, 1955, another unanimous decision of the Court, written by Chief Justice Warren, was handed down. On the basic question of integration, it held to the 1954 position. But on the question of how fast integration should be achieved, it compromised.

"It should go without saying," the opinion stated, "that constitutional principles cannot be allowed to yield simply because of disagreement with them." But applying them to local conditions was best done by local school boards, and local courts were in the best position to check up on them. "A prompt and reasonable start toward full compliance" must be made. But "once such a start has been made, the courts may find that additional time is necessary." Just how much additional time was for them to decide. They were instructed by the Supreme Court "to enter such orders and decrees . . . as are necessary and proper to admit to public schools on a racially non-discriminatory basis *with all deliberate speed* the parties to this case."

As this book is written, "all deliberate speed" has not—in nearly twenty years—carried out that directive. Worse, a new form of segregation has been growing while the old forms have been slowly whittled down.

White families who could afford to have moved out of the crowded centers of northern and western cities, leaving a majority of poor blacks in what are called "ghetto schools." De facto segregation—that is, segregation resulting from circumstances rather than that enforced by law—has become common in suburban schools.

White parents in northern middle-class communities have resisted the entrance of blacks into "their" schools as fiercely as white parents in Little Rock and Nashville resisted in the 1950's.

The 1955 decision did not accomplish what was hoped: the putting into effect of the principles of the 1954 decision without serious conflict in the communities that had to change, or damage to the prestige of the Court. There were bombings and burnings and murders in the years that followed. The schools of Prince Edward County were closed for four long years. In almost all cases it was blacks who suffered most. But not even Supreme Court justices were immune. For the rest of his long term in office Earl Warren had to face demands for his impeachment, and Justice Black was denounced so bitterly in the South that it was thirteen years before he made an official visit home.

What matters more is that our children are not yet "coming up together." * We have not yet made it possible for "our future citizens to learn their first lesson to respect the rights of the individual in a democracy." **

* From Silas Fleming's testimony, cf. p. 4.

** From Judge Waring's dissenting opinion in *Briggs* v. *Elliott*.

Bibliography
of Sources

Greenberg, Jack. *Race Relations and American Law.* New York: Columbia University Press, 1959.

Greenberg, Jack, and Hill, Herbert. *Citizen's Guide to Desegregation.* Boston: Beacon Press, 1955.

Smith, Bob. *They Closed Their Schools: Prince Edward County, Virginia, 1951–1964.* Chapel Hill: University of North Carolina Press, 1965.

Supreme Court Records Staff, Friedman, Leon, ed. *Argument: The Complete Oral Argument before the Supreme Court in Brown* vs. *Board of Education of Topeka, Kansas, 1952–1955.* New York: Chelsea House, 1969.

Briefs submitted in amicus curiae, by Herbert Brownell for the Department of Justice, 1954. (Available in law libraries that are depositories of Supreme Court documents.)

The Felix Frankfurter and Harold Burton papers. Washington: Library of Congress.

Various issues for the years 1950–1955:

> *The New York Times*
> *The Charleston News-Courier*
> *The Omaha Star*
> *The Chicago Defender*
> *The Richmond News Leader*
> *The Baltimore* (and *Richmond*) *Afro-American*

Index

Alabama, 23
Amici curiae, defined, 21

Banks, W. Lester, 12, 13
Belton, Ethel, 43
Belton v. *Gebhart*, 43
Black, Hugo, 48, 56, 57
Bledsoe, Charles, 39*n*.
Bolling, Spottswood Thomas, 44
Bolling v. *Sharpe*, 46
Brief, defined, 21*n*.
Briggs v. Elliott, 25*n*., 27–32 *passim*, 41, 42, 57*n*.
Brown, John, 33
Brown, Oliver, 39
Brown v. *Board of Education of Topeka*, 33–41 *passim*, 49
Bulah, Shirley, 43
Bulah v. *Gebhart*, 43
Bussing, school, 33, 39, 41

Caldwell, Herman, 34, 37, 38
Carper, Katherine, 41
Carter, Robert, 39*n*.
Charleston (S.C.), 15, 27, 29, 30
Civil War, 19
Clarendon County (S.C.), 15, 16–18, 28, 29, 30, 31, 32
Claymont (Del.), 43
Constitution, U.S., 19, 22, 27, 31
Court of Appeals for D.C. circuit, U.S., 46

Davis, John W., 48 and *n*.
Davis v. *County School Board*, 42
Delaware, 44
Desegregation, 12, 13, 24
    white resistance to, 13
    See also Segregation
District of Columbia, 10, 44, 46, 47, 54

Effects of Segregation and the Consequences of Desegregation, The, 47
Eisenhower, Dwight D., 47

Farmville (Va.), 1, 2, 8, 9, 12, 14
Farmville (Va.) High School, 13
Farmville (Va.) School Board, 3, 13, 42
Fifth Amendment, 46
First Baptist Church (Farmville), 8, 14
Fleming, Silas, 41, 57*n*.
Florida, 23
Fourteenth Amendment, 19, 21, 27, 49, 50
Frankfurter, Felix, 48

Garrett, Henry E., 42
Georgia, 23, 54
Goldberg, Arthur, 50*n*.
Greenberg, Jack, 39*n*., 44*n*.
Griffin, Francis, 8, 9, 10

Harlan, John Marshall, 53*n.*
Hayes, George E. C., 44*n.*
Hill, Oliver, 9, 10, 12, 13*n.*, 15
Hockessin (Del.), 43
Huxman, Walter, 41

Jackson, Robert, 48 and *n.*, 53 and *n.*
Johns, Barbara, 2, 3, 4, 5, 7, 10, 12, 14
Johns, Vernon, 8 and *n.*
Jones, Boyd, 1, 2, 4, 5, 7

Kansas, 10, 33, 43
King, Martin Luther, 8*n.*

Liberty Hill Elementary School, 16

McIlwaine, Superintendent, 8, 9
McLaurin, G. W., 18, 19, 21, 22, 23
Marshall, Thurgood, 25, 28, and *n.*, 29, 30, 31, 47–48
Menninger Foundation, 38 and *n.*
Mississippi, 23, 54
Montgomery (Ala.), 8 and *n.*
Moton High School (Farmville), 1, 2, 3, 4, 5, 7, 10, 13, 14, 15, 42

NAACP (National Association for the Advancement of Colored People), 4 and *n.*, 7, 8, 9, 12, 13, 17, 23, 37, 48
    and desegregation cases, 13, 25, 26, 27, 28, 29, 32, 37, 38
Nabrit, James M., Jr., 44*n.*
New York Times, 27

Office of Education, U.S., 25
Oklahoma, University of, 19

Parker, John J., 27, 31, 32
Parks, Rosa, 8*n.*
Pervall, J. B., 14, 15
Plessy v. *Ferguson*, 21, 24, 25, 26, 31, 41, 44, 50, 53
Prince Edward County (Va.), 1–15 *passim*, 24*n.*, 42, 57
    demand for desegregation in, 12
Pulaski County (Va.), 9, 10, 12, 13*n.*

Ram Bay Elementary School, 16
Redding, Louis L., 43, 44
Richmond (Va.), 9, 10, 15
Richmond (Va.) *Afro-American*, 17*n.*
Richmond (Va.) *News-Leader*, 18*n.*, 23*n.*
Robinson, Spottswood, 9, 10, 12, 13*n.*, 15

Scott, Charles, 37, 39*n.*
Scott, Elisha, 37
Scott, John, 37, 39*n.*
Scott's Branch Union School, 17
Segregation
    de facto, 56–57
    de jure, 21
    effects of, on school children, 30, 41
    See also Desegregation
Seitz, Collins J., 44
"Separate but equal" doctrine, 21, 24

Smalls, Robert, 31

Smith, Bob, 5n.

South Carolina, 10, 23, 26, 43, 54
    Marshall's attack on segregation law in, 31

Stokes, John, 5n.

Supreme Court, U.S., 10, 18, 19, 21, 23, 26, 28 and n., 31, 32, 37, 46, 47, 49, 50, 53, 54, 56, 57
    and *Brown* v. *Board of Education of Topeka*, 38n., 49
    and *Plessy* v. *Ferguson*, 21, 24, 25, 26, 31, 41, 44, 50, 53

Sweatt, Herman Marion, 18, 19, 21, 22, 23

Texas, University of, 19, 22

They Closed Their Schools, 5n.

Timmerman, George Bell, 27, 32

Todd, Alvin, 38

Todd, Lucinda, 37, 38

Topeka (Kans.), 33, 37

Vinson, Fred, 21, 22, 50

Virginia, 10, 54

Waring, Waites J., 25n., 27 and n., 28, 29n., 32, 57n.

Warren, Earl, 50, 53, 56, 57

Washington, D.C., 10, 44, 46, 47, 54

Wilmington (Del.), 43

About the Author

Janet Stevenson was born in Chicago and educated at Bryn Mawr and the Yale Drama School. While living in Hollywood, she wrote an original screenplay, *Weep No More*, which later became a play and then a novel. Two more novels followed, *The Ardent Years* and *Sisters and Brothers*. Mrs. Stevenson has also written a number of books for young people reflecting her interest in those struggling for their civil rights today. Two of these books are *Women's Rights* and *The Montgomery Bus Boycott*. The author, who is widowed and the mother of two sons, lives and writes in a house in the woods near Astoria, Oregon.